Harriet Tubman

Tubman sat for this photograph in Auburn, New York, during the late 1860s. Her face reveals the effect that years of hardship and backbreaking work had on her long life.

JUNIOR ■ WORLD ■ BIOGRAPHIES

Harriet Tubman

BREE BURNS

CHELSEA JUNIORS

a division of CHELSEA HOUSE PUBLISHERS

Chelsea House Publishers
EDITOR-IN-CHIEF: Remmel Nunn
MANAGING EDITOR: Karyn Gullen Browne
COPY CHIEF: Mark Rifkin
PICTURE EDITOR: Adrian G. Allen
ART DIRECTOR: Maria Epes
ASSISTANT ART DIRECTOR: Howard Brotman
MANUFACTURING DIRECTOR: Gerald Levine
SYSTEMS MANAGER: Lindsey Ottman
PRODUCTION MANAGER: Joseph Romano
PRODUCTION COORDINATOR: Marie Claire Cebrián

JUNIOR WORLD BIOGRAPHIES

SENIOR EDITOR: Kathy Kuhtz

Staff for HARRIET TUBMAN
SENIOR COPY EDITOR: Laurie Kahn
EDITORIAL ASSISTANT: Karen Akins
PICTURE RESEARCHER: Ellen Barrett
SENIOR DESIGNER: Marjorie Zaum
COVER ILLUSTRATION: Vilma Ortiz

7   9   8   6

Library of Congress Cataloging-in-Publication Data
Burns, Bree.
    Harriet Tubman/Bree Burns.
        p.   cm.—(Junior world biographies)
    Includes index.
    Summary: A biography of the Afro-American woman best known for her
work with the Underground Railroad, describing her childhood as a slave, her
escape to the North, her work during the Civil War, and more.
    ISBN   0-7910-1751-6   0-7910-1995-0 (pbk.)
    1. Tubman, Harriet, 1820?–1913—Juvenile literature.   2. Slaves—United
States—Biography—Juvenile literature.   3. Afro-Americans—Biography—
Juvenile literature.   [1. Tubman, Harriet, 1820?–1913.   2. Afro-
Americans—Biography.   3. Underground railroad   4. Slaves.]   I. Title.
II. Series.
E444.T82B87   1992   91-28383
973′.049607302—dc20   CIP
[B]   AC

Contents

Harriet Tubman holds a musket in this engraving, but she usually carried a pistol during her trips on the Underground Railroad.

1

A Life for Freedom

Harriet Tubman was a runaway slave who worked most of her life to eliminate slavery in the United States. She grew up in the 19th century, born into one of the cruelest systems of slavery ever created by humans.

As early as the 16th century, African and European slave traders began stealing people from Africa to do heavy labor in the European colonies around the world. The first slaves in the British colonies of North America arrived on a Dutch ship and were sold at Jamestown, Virginia, in 1619. Before President Abraham Lincoln officially freed the slaves in the Southern states in 1863, millions of men, women, and children had been kidnapped from their homes in Africa and were sold on the *auction* block, like farm animals, to the highest bidder.

The people who suffered the long, horrible voyage, known as the middle passage, across the Atlantic Ocean were chained by their wrists and ankles and crowded onto ships. Many of the African captives threw themselves overboard and drowned during the trip so that they would not have to live as slaves. Often the ship's captain would not allow the Africans up on the deck because he did not want to lose his precious cargo to the sea. Instead, the Africans suffocated in the heat and darkness below, in the cargo holds of the ships. Many others died from hunger or thirst or from diseases they caught from eating the rotten food and drinking salty water. When they finally reached port in the colonies, the Africans

Chained captives were crowded onto the ships that made the voyage across the Atlantic Ocean, a journey known as the middle passage. Many people died from starvation and disease during the journey.

were unloaded into dockside slave pens. They were cleaned and then fattened for a few weeks, just like cattle. Sometimes they were even branded with red-hot irons. They were stripped naked and sold at auctions. Frequently, children were separated from their parents and sold to *plantation* owners far away. Many times families were kept apart forever. The men who sold Africans as slaves became very wealthy.

Many blacks were born into slavery in America. Harriet Tubman, whose parents were full-blooded Africans, was born on a Maryland plantation in about 1820. In 1849, she escaped to freedom in the North, where the antislavery movement was strong. Risking her life, she returned to the South many times to help hundreds of other slaves who were not afraid to flee. She bravely guided them along the Underground Railroad, which was not a railroad in the usual sense. It did not have trains or tracks. The Underground Railroad was the name given to a network of people willing to hide runaway slaves in their homes. Those who helped the runaways reach their next Underground Railroad station—a safe house or barn to hide in—were also very daring. The authorities severely punished people who helped slaves escape.

According to one legend, the Underground Railroad got its name during the pursuit of a runaway slave in Kentucky. When the slave jumped into the Ohio River and desperately began to swim, his owner, or master, followed closely behind in a boat. By the time his owner reached the shore, the slave had disappeared. The frustrated slave owner reportedly cried, "He must have gone on an underground railroad!"

The fleeing slaves hiked through woods and swamps, hiding in barns, houses, and ditches. Slave owners sent men with guns to hunt for them. There were large rewards offered for Harriet's capture because she had helped so many slaves escape bondage.

But if Harriet Tubman was ever afraid during these dangerous trips, people said she did not show it. She believed very strongly in what she was doing to help other black people. Even as a young person, Harriet showed her bravery and willingness to help other slaves. Once, when she was 15 years old, she was shucking corn with the other slaves on the plantation. She noticed a tall black man creeping away from the group. The overseer, who had been hired to watch the slaves and make sure they did not escape, chased the man. Harriet followed them.

Catching up with the running slave at a store down the road, the overseer prepared to whip him. The overseer saw Harriet and asked her to help him while he tied the slave down. She refused. The runaway slave fled, and Harriet blocked the overseer's way. Angered, he grabbed a two-pound lead weight from the store shelf and threw it after the running slave. It missed its target and hit Harriet instead. She fell down hard. Blood poured from the wound on her head.

Harriet was carried home to the plantation. Her terrified mother bandaged her head, but the teenager was in a coma for many weeks and lay on a bed of rags in her family's small cabin. She could not walk for many months. No doctor was asked to examine her because the slave owner did not want to spend money on medical treatment. Many slave owners did not "waste" doctors on their slaves. Harriet probably had a fractured skull and a *concussion*. Eventually, a scar marked her forehead. For the rest of her life, Harriet Tubman suffered "sleeping fits" as a result of her injury. Sometimes she would fall asleep when she was talking and could not be awakened.

When Harriet did not work as a conductor, or guide, on the Underground Railroad, she worked with the *abolitionist* movement. An abolitionist was a person who strove to abolish, or end, slavery in the United States. As slavery spread in the South, emotion against it began to grow in the North, where the economy had turned toward manufacturing instead of farming. As its need for slave labor lessened, each northern state outlawed slavery. Many people in the North felt it was morally wrong for one human being to own another. The conflict over slavery came to a head in 1860–61, when 11 Southern states rebelled, separating from the North to form their own country. The Civil War between the Confederate States of America (the South) and the Union (the North) began in 1861.

An 1835 leaflet, published by the American Anti-Slavery Society, shows a slave asking, "Am I not a man and a brother?" The abolitionists felt it was morally wrong for one human being to own another.

During the Civil War, Harriet Tubman served as a nurse for the Union soldiers. She also spied on Confederate troops for the North by leading a small group of Union scouts into enemy territory and returning with information about the location of Confederate camps. In 1865, the Union defeat of the Confederates put an end to the practice of slavery.

Harriet Tubman's life story is an inspiration to blacks and women in their ongoing battle for equal rights. She is remembered as a hero who was not afraid to fight for her beliefs. Tubman's dedication to justice has become a model for all Americans. Tubman was respected by many people during her lifetime. They showed their esteem by giving her the nickname Moses, after the biblical prophet who led his people, the Israelites, out of slavery in Egypt to freedom in the Promised Land.

The Virginia slave Nat Turner led 60 slaves in a revolt against their white masters in 1831. News of the rebellion swept the Brodas plantation, where Harriet lived, and filled the slaves with excitement and pride.

2

A Childhood in Slavery

Harriet Ross was born in about 1820 in Maryland's Dorchester County on the Eastern Shore. The Eastern Shore is part of the Delmarva Peninsula, which lies between the Chesapeake and Delaware bays and includes parts of the states of Delaware, Maryland, and Virginia. The rich farmland of the Eastern Shore is known as the Tidewater because its inlets, swamps, and small rivers rise and fall with the tides of the nearby Atlantic Ocean.

Usually, no official records were kept on the birth of slaves at that time, so Harriet's birthdate is approximate. Because few slaves could read or write, they could not keep their own records. Harriet was one of 11 children born to the slaves Harriet Green and Benjamin Ross, who belonged to the planter Edward Brodas. Both of her parents came from the Ashanti tribe, a West African warrior tribe. Harriet's mother, who was called Old Rit, gave her daughter the "cradle name" of Araminta. Until Harriet became a teenager, her family called her Minty.

Edward Brodas planted apples, wheat, rye, and corn on his plantation. On his land grew oak, cypress, and poplar trees, and he sold the lumber from these trees to the Baltimore shipyards across the bay. Like many slave owners of the Upper South, Brodas bred and raised blacks as a cash crop, renting and selling them to others. Harriet's father, who was called Old Ben, spent most of his days cutting timber for his master. Harriet's mother worked for the Brodas family in their el-

A southern planter shouts an order to his field slaves.
Edward Brodas, Harriet's master, planted many crops
on his land, but he also raised blacks as a cash crop,
renting and selling them to others.

egant home, which the slaves referred to as "the big house."

Harriet's master rented her out as a laborer to a local couple named Cook when she was five years old. At the Cooks' home, the little girl slept on the floor. Whenever it got cold, Harriet put her feet under the ashes in the fireplace to keep warm. She shared scraps of food with the Cooks' dogs. When it turned out that she wound yarn too slowly for his wife, who was a weaver, Mr. Cook ordered Harriet to watch muskrat traps instead. She spent her days wading barefoot in the icy river, looking for muskrats on traplines. Later, when she developed a cough and high fever, Cook accused her of faking her illness to avoid work. The Cooks sent her back to the Brodas plantation, where Harriet recovered from an attack of measles and bronchitis. Then Brodas rented Harriet to a woman who wanted a housekeeper and someone to care for her baby.

Many years after the episode, Harriet described it to a friend:

I was only seven years old when I was sent away to take care of a baby. . . . And that baby was always on my lap except when it was asleep or when its mother was feeding it.

One morning, after breakfast [she] had the baby, and I stood by the table waiting until I was to take it; near me was a bowl of lumps of white sugar. My mistress got into a great quarrel with her husband; she had an awful temper. . . . That sugar . . . did look so nice, and my mistress's back was turned to me while she was fighting with her husband, so I just put my fingers in the sugar bowl to take one lump and maybe she heard me for she turned and saw me. The next minute she had the rawhide down. I gave one jump out of the door and I saw that they came after me, but I just flew and they didn't catch me. I ran and I ran . . . but I didn't dare to stop. . . .

By and by when I was almost tuckered out, I came to a great big pigpen. There was an old sow there, and perhaps eight or ten little pigs. I tumbled over . . . [the pen] . . . and fell in . . . so beaten out that I could not stir.

And there I stayed from Friday until the next Tuesday, fighting with those little pigs for the potato peelings and the other scraps that came down in the trough. The old sow would push me away when I tried to get her children's food, and I was awfully afraid of her.

By Tuesday I was so starved I knew I had to go back to my mistress. I didn't have anywhere else to go, even though I knew what was coming. So I went back.

Harriet returned to her mistress, who whipped her and brought her back to the Brodas plantation. Old Rit nursed Harriet, salving the fresh wounds on top of the scars from earlier beatings. As soon as Harriet was able to work, Brodas hired her out again. This time she was put to work splitting fence rails and loading timber onto wagons. It was backbreaking work, better suited to a man than to a little girl. But Harriet preferred working outdoors.

By the time she was in her early teens, Harriet was known as a strong but surly laborer, unfit for indoor work but useful as a field hand. She never forgot her childhood and never had a good word for any of her masters. If they had any excuse for their cruelty, she believed, it was their ignorance. "They didn't know any better. It's the way they were brought up . . . with the whip in their hand," she said years later.

In 1831, when Harriet was about 11, exciting news was passed around the slave quarters of the Brodas estate. Nat Turner, a slave on a Virginia plantation—only 100 miles away, across the Chesapeake Bay—had led an army of about 60 rebel slaves against their white masters. More than 50 whites had been killed in the uprising. Turner and his men had lost the battle, but the revolt proved that slaves were human beings, not animals, and that they were willing to fight and die for freedom.

There had been other uprisings by blacks in the South. In 1800, a Virginia slave named

Gabriel Prosser had tried, but failed, to establish an independent black state. And in 1822, Denmark Vesey had organized hundreds of blacks in a spectacular but unsuccessful attempt at winning freedom in South Carolina. These rebellions sparked hope among the South's blacks and fear among the whites.

Slaves found other ways to establish a certain degree of independence. Some pretended to be stupid, "accidentally" destroying their master's tools and crops. Others escaped when they had a chance, but escape was usually very difficult. The standard punishment for runaways was to whip them, brand them with the letter *R*, and exile them to the Deep South, where working conditions for slaves were more brutal than anywhere else. Slaves who were sent to Louisiana or Georgia hardly ever came back; many died shortly after being sent there.

Harriet had developed a reputation for defiance and rebellion, especially after the incident in which she was hit in the head while trying to help a runaway slave. Brodas decided to sell her and two of her brothers to someone in the Deep South. Before he could sell them, however, Brodas fell ill and died. The next man who ran the estate decided that rather than send her away, he would rent Harriet out to John Stewart, a local builder.

Stewart was so impressed with Harriet's energy and will to work that he allowed her a privilege that was given to only the most trusted slaves: When times were slow on the farm, she could hire herself out to other people to make her own money. In return, she paid him about $50 each year; any money she earned above that was hers to keep. For the next five years, she cut timber for Stewart and, in her spare time, chopped and hauled wood for neighbors. Slowly she was able to save a small amount of money.

Harriet liked outdoor work, and she liked being able to earn her own money. Still, she did not have what she felt to be the most important right in the world—freedom—and it existed for her only 90 miles to the north.

A Maryland slave owner posted this notice offering
$100 for the return of his runaway "servant."

$100 REWARD.

Ran away from my farm, near Buena Vista P. O., Prince George's County, Maryland, on the first day of April, 1855, my servant MATHEW TURNER.

He is about five feet six or eight inches high; weighs from one hundred and sixty to one hundred and eighty pounds; he is very black, and has a remarkably thick upper lip and neck; looks as if his eyes are half closed; walks slow, and talks and laughs loud.

I will give One Hundred Dollars reward to whoever will secure him in jail, so that I get him again, no matter where taken.

MARCUS DU VAL.

BUENA VISTA P. O., MD.,
MAY 10, 1855.

3

A Daring Escape
to the North

In the South, slaves began to fight back at their oppressors. In the North, free blacks took up the abolitionist cause with passion. Blacks and their white supporters had been highly impressed by the actions of Toussaint L'Ouverture, a former slave who in 1791 led a revolution in Haiti, which was then called St. Domingue. After freeing Haiti's black slaves, Toussaint forced the British and Spanish out of their positions of power and established the Western Hemisphere's first black republic.

Another model of gallant actions in the fight for the abolition of slavery was David Walker, a free black Bostonian. In 1829, he published *Appeal*, a strongly worded pamphlet that urged the slaves of the South to rise in rebellion against their white masters. Some historians believe that Walker's powerful arguments had inspired Nat Turner to revolt in 1831.

William Lloyd Garrison, a white journalist and reformer in Massachusetts, became an important leader of the abolitionist movement. Garrison, who founded the journal *The Liberator* in 1831, took a highly unusual stand on the issue, calling for the immediate abolition of slavery. Most abolitionists favored freeing slaves gradually and then paying the slave owners for the loss of their "property."

Frederick Douglass, another important leader in the antislavery movement, was born on Maryland's Eastern Shore in 1818. After escaping to New York in 1838, he went to Massachusetts and became an agent of the Anti-Slavery Society

Frederick Douglass, a runaway slave, became an important leader in the fight to end slavery. He lectured for the American Anti-Slavery Society and later published an abolitionist paper called the North Star.

and gave lectures on the abolition of slavery. He founded an abolitionist newspaper, the *North Star*, later called *Frederick Douglass's Paper*. Over the years, Douglass recruited thousands of people to the abolitionist cause.

In 1839, news of a daring act at sea struck hope into the hearts of all those who were against slavery. An African named Joseph Cinque led the black captives of a Spanish slave ship, the *Amistad*, in a revolt in which they hijacked the ship. After killing most of the Spanish crew, the rebels sailed the ship to the coast of Long Island, New York. There they were arrested and jailed on charges of piracy and murder. They eventually won their freedom in court and returned to their homes in Africa.

The *Amistad* case caused a lot of excitement among both blacks and whites. Harriet and the other slaves at the Brodas plantation had probably heard about the brave act. They longed for their own freedom.

In 1844, John Tubman, a free black man

who lived in a cabin near the Brodas plantation, asked 24-year-old Harriet Ross to marry him. She accepted his proposal. Because his slave parents had been freed after their master's death, John Tubman had been born a free man. Marriage to a free man, however, did not mean Harriet Tubman was free; it meant only that she was allowed to share her husband's cabin late at night. She was still a slave. Her children, if she had any, would belong to the Brodas estate.

While she was married, Tubman learned that she was being held in slavery illegally, according to the laws of Maryland. Her mother, Old Rit, often said that she had been promised freedom years earlier but was cheated out of it. Over the years, Tubman had managed to save five dollars, and in 1845, she took it to a local lawyer and asked him to look into her mother's records for her.

The lawyer discovered that Old Rit's owner had specified in his will that she be freed upon reaching the age of 45. But upon her owner's death Old Rit had been sold to someone else, despite the statement in the will. The lawyer told Tubman that she and her mother were legally free. However, he said, because so much time had passed and because the women had always lived as slaves, no judge would even consider the case. So it seemed that Tubman was doomed to live the rest of her life as a slave.

As a result of her childhood injury, Tubman continued to suffer blackouts, during which she often had strange and frightening dreams. She described them later as scenes from the horrifying middle passage, the Atlantic crossing that cost the lives of millions of captive Africans on the way to America. Although Harriet had never made this journey herself, she dreamed of ships where blacks and whites fought on decks stained with blood. She also dreamed about a mother clutching a baby to her breast and jumping into the sea to her death.

Even during her marriage, Tubman lived in fear of being "sold South," and in 1849 her worst fears came true. The owner of the Brodas estate died, and word spread that his guardian planned to settle the plantation's bills by selling some of its slaves. Tubman knew it was time to run away to freedom. She told her brothers what she had heard about the Underground Railroad and about the people in the North who would help them. Her father had shown her how to use the North Star at night as a *compass*; she told her brothers that she could guide them north by watching it.

Harriet did not want to leave her husband, but she knew better than to ask him to come along or even tell him about her plan. He had already promised to betray her if she ever tried to escape. She left late at night with her brothers, but the men soon began to have second thoughts about running away. They were worried about what would happen to them when it was discovered that they were missing. Signs would be posted everywhere, and alarm bells would ring. Dogs would be set loose to hunt for them, and patrollers with whips would track them down. They became afraid and decided to turn back. They made Tubman go back with them.

Two days after they returned home, Harriet Tubman received bad news: She had been sold and was to be sent south the next day. This time, she knew she would have to try to escape alone. Years later, she described her thoughts at the moment she made her decision: "There was one of two things I had a *right* to, liberty or death; if I could not have one, I would have the other; for no man should take me alive; I should fight for my liberty as long as my strength lasted, and when the time came for me to go, the Lord would let them take me."

Tubman wanted someone in her family to know she was leaving on her own, that she had not been taken south. After her last experience, she would not tell her brothers. Legend has it that she made her way toward the big house, where one of her sisters was working in the kitchen. Walking back and forth near the window, Harriet sang an old *spiritual* hymn:

I'll meet you in the morning,
When I reach the Promised Land,
On the other side of Jordan.
For I'm bound for the Promised Land.

That night, after her husband had gone to sleep, Tubman wrapped up a little corn bread and salt herring, then tucked her favorite patchwork quilt under her arm. She made her way through the woods to the house of a local white woman who, it was said, helped runaways. When Tubman arrived at the door, the woman seemed to know what her visitor wanted. She invited Tubman in, then gave her two slips of paper, explaining that each contained the name of a family that lived along the road north. When Harriet presented the slips, said the woman, these people would feed her and tell her how to get to the next house. These slips of paper were Harriet's first "tickets" on the Underground Railroad. As an expression of her gratitude for the woman's help, Tubman gave the woman her favorite quilt.

Reaching the first house just after dawn,

Tubman gave a woman there the first slip of paper. The woman responded by giving Tubman a broom and telling her to sweep the walk. At first Tubman was shocked by the order. Then she realized that this was meant to be a disguise: A black woman hard at work sweeping would never be suspected as a runaway slave by a passerby.

Runaways from Louisiana rest during their flight to freedom in the North. Many runaways feared that dogs and patrollers with whips would be sent to track them down.

As soon as night fell, the woman's husband asked Tubman to climb into the back of his farm wagon. He covered her with vegetables and drove her north to the next "station." In this way, sometimes helped by others and sometimes left to her own devices, Harriet Tubman made her way north, walking through the Eastern Shore toward the state of Pennsylvania. She carefully learned the route that she would come to use so well in the future.

Traveling by night and hiding during the day, Tubman hiked through 90 miles of swamp and woodland. Finally, she found herself north of the *Mason-Dixon line*, the boundary between Pennsylvania and Maryland. The Mason-Dixon line became known as the border between the slave states of the South and the free states of the North. Years later, Tubman commented about the day she made the crossing: "I looked at my hands to see if I was the same person now that I was free. There was such a glory over everything; the sun came like gold through the trees, and over the fields, and I felt like I was in heaven."

Philadelphia, Pennsylvania, was home to many abolitionists. Harriet escaped to freedom and arrived there in 1849.

4

The Brave Conductor

Harriet Tubman's first stop as a free woman was in Philadelphia, Pennsylvania, where she worked washing dishes in a hotel kitchen, saved her money, and thought about how she could help her family back in Maryland. Years later, she said: "To this solemn resolution I came. I was free, and [my parents, brothers, and sisters] should be free also."

Many abolitionists lived in Philadelphia. Blacks and whites there had been unified against the passage of the Fugitive Slave Act of 1850. Under this federal law, any black accused of being a runaway could be brought before a federal judge or a special commissioner. Denied a jury trial or the right to testify on their own behalf, the alleged runaways could easily be returned to slavery. All that was required to make an accusation was a sworn statement from a white person who claimed to be the black person's owner. The law also set up strict penalties for anyone who helped a slave escape. Many northerners were offended by the Fugitive Slave Act, believing that it violated the principles of the U.S. Constitution and basic human rights. Whenever they could, the abolitionists worked against the Fugitive Slave Act.

Soon after the act was passed by Congress, Tubman made her first trip back across the Mason-Dixon line to Baltimore, Maryland. One night she visited the office of the Vigilance Committee, which had been formed to help runaway slaves escape and was managed by two of the Underground Railroad's busiest "station masters," white clergyman James Miller McKim and freeborn black Pennsylvanian William Still. While Tubman called upon the committee's officials, a visitor asked her for help. He explained that the husband of a slave family, who was a free man, wanted to bring the rest of his family to the North. The family, which was in Cambridge, Maryland, needed someone to act as a guide. As the visitor described the escape plan, he mentioned the name of the free man: John Bowley. Tubman probably looked startled when she heard the name spoken; Bowley was her brother-in-law, the husband of her sister Mary.

Over the objections of her friends McKim and Still, Tubman insisted that she help her own family. She was a fugitive, or runaway, herself, and it would be dangerous, but Harriet knew the land and she could leave immediately. The timing of the escape was critical because Mary Bowley and her children were going to be sold on the auction block soon. If Bowley could bring Mary and her children as far as Baltimore, Tubman would guide them the rest of the way to Philadelphia.

When Tubman and her companions got to Maryland, Bowley went on to the auction in Cambridge. Posing as a slave who belonged to the auctioneer, Bowley presented the guards with a letter requesting that the female captive, Mary, and her children be turned over to him. The slaves were to be taken to a hotel where the auctioneer was having lunch.

Bowley marched his family through the streets of Cambridge to the home of a helpful *Quaker* family. They hid in the house until the next day, when they were all put on a small sailboat that was headed north to Baltimore. When Bowley spotted the prearranged signal, one blue and one yellow lantern, he knew that it would be safe to bring the sailboat ashore. A white woman met the fugitives, hid them among a wagonload of potatoes, and then drove them to a brick house. Bowley knocked on the door, and a voice from inside said, "Who's there?" He responded with

Conductors on the Underground Railroad cautiously help runaways escape to freedom. This painting portrays the seriousness of the abolitionists' work—there were severe penalties for people who were caught helping slaves escape.

the Underground Railroad password: "A friend with friends." The door opened, and Tubman rushed out to hug her family. Tubman conducted her family along the Underground Railroad, and they made it back to Philadelphia safely, as Tubman would always do on her journeys for the Railroad. "I never ran my train off the track," she said years later, "and I never lost a passenger." During her lifetime, she made more than 19 trips to the South, helping more than 300 slaves escape.

On her second trip to the South, Harriet Tubman rescued her two brothers and helped some other men escape. On her third trip, she returned to the Brodas plantation, to her husband's cabin. She knocked on the door. John Tubman opened it. He had a new wife, he told her, and he had no interest in going anywhere. Harriet left the plantation and never looked back. She never saw her husband again, and she rarely spoke about him.

When she made her trips south, Tubman usually gathered money and supplies in the North and then slipped down to the Eastern Shore, through Delaware and into Maryland. There she would make contact with the slaves who were ready to escape. She usually led slaves away from captivity on a Saturday, during the night, hoping that they would not be missed until Monday. Once they left on their trip, the slaves knew there would be no turning back. Slaves who returned to their owners were cruelly beaten until they told the names of the abolitionists who had helped them. More than once, a slave grew fainthearted and wanted to go back home, as Tubman's brothers had the first time she tried to run away. But Tubman always carried a revolver with her. She would point it at the wavering slave's head and say, "Move or die!" None of her passengers ever turned back, and she never lost anyone during a journey.

Tubman's return route on her trips led her through Delaware as far as possible before crossing into Pennsylvania. Traveling through Delaware had a few advantages. First, it contained the headwaters of most of the rivers that drained the Eastern Shore, which meant that a small boat could be used to reach almost any point. Also, Delaware was home to many more free black women and men than slaves. It was the only state in the South where a black person was assumed to be free unless proven to be a slave.

On most of her trips, Tubman made her last stop Wilmington, Delaware, a city right on the Mason-Dixon line. It was the home of Thomas Garrett, a Quaker who became one of Harriet's closest friends. He owned a large shoe store and hid fleeing slaves behind a false wall in his shop. He also gave each runaway a pair of shoes, for many the first pair they had ever owned. According to William Still's records, Thomas Garrett helped approximately 2,700 slaves escape to freedom.

By 1851, the Fugitive Slave Act was taking a heavy toll on runaways. Fugitive slaves were being arrested and returned south from cities such as Boston, Massachusetts, and Syracuse, New York, which had previously been safe for them. Free blacks and white abolitionists in the North began to fight back. In Boston, 300 armed men were needed to send 1 fugitive back to the South. The Fugitive Slave Act backfired in the long run because it increased the North's opposition to slavery. But it did succeed in making life difficult for Harriet Tubman and the other conductors on the Underground Railroad. No longer able to work safely in Philadelphia, Tubman moved to St. Catharines, Canada, a small town near Niagara Falls where many free blacks and former slaves had settled. Between 1851 and 1857, she made two trips to the Eastern Shore each year, one in the fall and one in the spring. But now, instead of a trip about 90 miles long, she had to lead her passengers on a 500-mile-long journey.

Tubman became very good at disguising herself. Once, when she had to enter the village where her former master lived, she made herself look like an old slave who was bringing chickens to market. When she saw her old master coming toward her, she let the chickens loose and chased them to a nearby fence. Amid the laughter of the bystanders, her former master walked right by without recognizing her. On another occasion, she disguised herself by pretending to read a book. Hoping she was holding the book right side up, Tubman heard one man whisper to another: "This can't be the woman. The one we want can't read or write."

In late 1854, Harriet received word that three of her brothers, Benjamin, John, and William Henry, were going to be sold South the day after Christmas. Harriet had a friend write to a literate black man who lived near the estate where her brothers worked as hired slaves. "Read my letter to the old folks [Old Ben and Old Rit], and give my love to them. Tell my brothers to be always watching unto prayer, and when the good old ship of Zion comes along, be ready to step on board."

On Christmas Eve, Harriet arrived and collected her brothers, two other men, and a young woman. She would not take her parents on this trip, for she knew that because of their old age it was unlikely that they would be sold South. When Tubman and her charges arrived at Old Ben and Old Rit's cabin, they hid in an outbuilding where feed corn was stored. The parents knew nothing of the escape plan. Tubman longed to see her mother, but she knew the old woman was unable to keep a secret and would tell the whole neighborhood about their plan. Tubman sent her brothers and the two other men to the cabin; they called Old Ben outside and told him what was happening. He promised to keep the secret from Old Rit.

Ben Ross, a slave for almost 50 years, had earned a widespread reputation for his honesty. When he visited his children in the outbuilding, he turned his eyes away and never looked directly at them. When he said good-bye to them the next day, he had a bandanna tied over his eyes. A few days later, after Tubman and her passengers had headed north, a team of slave chasers questioned Old Ben and Old Rit about the runaways. They discovered that Old Rit was heartbroken because her sons had not shown up for Christmas. Old Ben said he had not laid eyes on his children, and the slave chasers believed the story. They knew Ben Ross was no liar.

John Brown, an antislavery crusader, met Harriet Tubman in 1858. Tubman had planned to assist Brown in his raid at Harpers Ferry the following year but fell ill and could not join him.

5

Harriet Goes to War

B<small>y</small> 1854, the woman called Moses was well known throughout the Eastern Shore. The authorities offered a $12,000 reward for Harriet Tubman's capture, and *bounty hunters* often searched for her. But Tubman could not be caught. William Still of the Vigilance Committee noted, "Great fears were entertained for her safety, but she seemed wholly devoid of personal fear. The idea of being captured by slave-hunters or slaveholders, seemed never to enter her mind." He thought that her "success into going to Maryland as she did was attributable to her adventurous spirit and utter disregard of consequences. Her like it is probable was never known before or since."

It was not until 1857 that Tubman was able to help Old Ben and Old Rit escape. Slipping into her parents' cabin late one night, she told them to get ready for the trip north. Next, she daringly walked over to a plantation stable, found a horse, and hitched it to a rickety wagon. Three days later, she and her parents arrived in Wilmington, Delaware.

Harriet Tubman's work on the Underground Railroad always involved cunning and secrecy. She sometimes lectured at abolitionist meetings but really preferred to work in a more private way. However, after Tubman caught the attention of the abolitionist John Brown, she lost any chance of *not* becoming well known. Brown believed that God had chosen him to destroy the institution of slavery. He planned to take up arms, if necessary, to force an end to the practice everywhere.

Congress had passed the Kansas-Nebraska Act in 1854, which stirred up savage conflict between proslavery and antislavery forces in Kansas Territory. The law had established the Kansas and Nebraska territories and gave the settlers in these lands the right, when they applied for statehood, to vote on whether their state would become a slave state or a free state. In the late 1850s, Brown and his followers attacked the proslavery settlement of Pottawatomie in Kansas in revenge for an attack on the antislavery town of Lawrence. As a result of the 2 raids, civil conflict broke out in Kansas, and more than 200 settlers died in the warfare. (In 1861, Kansas voted to enter the Union as a free state.)

John Brown met Harriet Tubman in 1858, and he asked her to help guide slaves through the Underground Railroad to his headquarters near Harpers Ferry, Virginia. He also asked her to help him recruit free blacks for a battle he was planning against proslavery forces there. On the night of October 16, 1859, Brown led his small force into Harpers Ferry and seized the federal arsenal, where the government's ammunition was stored. The local militia and a company of marines led by Colonel Robert E. Lee defeated Brown and his comrades. Several of Brown's men were killed, including two of his sons. A Virginia court tried Brown and his men, convicted them of *treason* and murder, and later hanged them. Tubman had planned to help Brown fight at Harpers Ferry, but she became sick and could not join him. Tubman was deeply saddened by Brown's death.

By the following spring, Tubman had recovered from her illness and began to work again. In April 1860, she staged her own raid, overwhelming scores of lawmen and rescuing fugitive slave Charles Nalle in Troy, New York. She also spent time in Boston, speaking to abolitionist groups.

Disagreement over slavery and states' rights continued to fuel the conflict between the North and the South. Southern states wanted no meddling in their state affairs by the federal government, especially regarding the issue of slavery.

In 1860, the rift between the North and the South worsened with the election of Abraham Lincoln as president of the United States. Because

Abraham Lincoln won the election for the office of president in 1860. Because he opposed the spread of slavery, Lincoln was looked upon as an enemy of the South.

Lincoln opposed the spread of slavery, he was looked upon by most southerners as an enemy. The Confederate States of America drew up their own constitution and elected their own president and vice-president. Confederate troops opened fire on Fort Sumter in Charleston, South Carolina, on April 12, 1861, beginning the Civil War.

As Union troops advanced through Maryland in 1861, large numbers of blacks left the

Newly freed slaves line up outside a contraband school. In April 1861, Tubman answered the call to help the contrabands in South Carolina, many of whom were sick and illiterate.

plantations to join the soldiers of the North. Officially called the "contraband of war," these blacks were no longer slaves but were not yet legally free. President Lincoln did not sign the Emancipation Proclamation, freeing the slaves of the South, until January 1, 1863.

In April 1861, Harriet Tubman headed south to help care for the *contrabands*. Little is known about her activities during this period.

When Union forces took Port Royal in South Carolina's Sea Islands, many illiterate, sick, and malnourished contrabands flooded the Union army camps. Overwhelmed by their numbers, the Union army sent out a call for help to teachers and nurses. Tubman answered the call, along with hundreds of others who volunteered.

When she arrived in South Carolina, Tubman discovered that she could barely communicate with the local black people. Still linked closely to Africa, these former slaves spoke a dialect (a variety of a language that is typical of a particular group of people or part of a country), and the dialect contained many African words. They were also very suspicious of whites and of those who worked for them. Tubman had to win her patients' confidence step-by-step. She worked at several Southern military hospitals, reporting when she was needed, then moving on.

Aware of Tubman's work on the Underground Railroad, the Union army in South Carolina soon gave her a new job: spy. They needed information about the number of enemy camps, where the camps were located, and how well the enemy's troops were armed. In the spring of 1863, Tubman organized a scouting service, leading a small band of black men deep into enemy territory and returning with information about Confederate troops.

Perhaps the most celebrated of Tubman's

On July 18, 1863, the 54th Massachusetts Infantry, a black unit of the Union army, attacks Fort Wagner in Charleston, South Carolina. After the tragic defeat of the black troops, Tubman helped nurse the wounded and bury the dead.

fearless missions took place in the summer of 1863. Tubman had to lead several gunboats up the Combahee River in South Carolina to remove mines placed there by the Confederates. She also had to guide hundreds of blacks out of the Confederate-held area. On the night of June 2, 1863, she and Colonel James Montgomery started up the river with 150 black soldiers in 3 steam-powered gunboats. The expedition, as the *Boston Commonwealth* later reported, "dashed into the enemy's country, struck a bold and effective blow, destroying millions of dollars worth of commis-

Harriet Tubman (far left) poses with former slaves in the North. The government never officially rewarded Tubman for her courageous and tireless work during the Civil War.

sary stores [which sell military provisions], cotton, and lordly dwellings, and striking terror into the heart of rebeldom, brought off near 800 slaves and thousands of dollars worth of property, without losing a man or receiving a scratch."

Tubman continued to perform important work during the war. She saw some of the bloodiest battles of the Civil War, such as the Union attack on Fort Wagner, which guarded the harbor at Charleston. The 54th Massachusetts Infantry, black soldiers commanded by a white officer, led the attack on July 18, 1863. The 54th Massachusetts lost the battle, its young commander, and about half its soldiers, but the battle marked the first important use of black troops in the war. Tubman helped nurse the wounded and bury those who had died during this battle.

For the next year, Harriet Tubman remained in the South. By taking part in numerous Union army operations, she earned the respect and admiration of the military. But Tubman was never officially thanked or paid a cent for her hard work.

In 1911, Harriet Tubman, seen here in probably the last photograph ever taken of her, moved into the home she had built for sick and elderly blacks. She once told a friend "of the sweet spirit in that home, and of the happiness she felt was there."

6

"This Most Wonderful Woman"

In May 1864, Harriet Tubman took a leave from her work at the Port Royal military hospital and went to Auburn, New York, to visit her parents. Once there, her years of nonstop work caught up with her; exhausted and ill, she suffered a bad bout of the sleeping seizures. She spent almost a year in Auburn, resting and visiting with her friends and neighbors. Then she moved to Washington, D.C., where she again worked as a nurse for the government.

On April 9, 1865, Confederate general Robert E. Lee surrendered to U.S. general Ulysses S. Grant at Appomattox, Virginia. A few months later, a tired and weary Harriet Tubman headed for home. The Civil War had ended. But for Harriet and millions of other free black Americans, another fight—the fight for equal civil rights—had just begun. (Civil rights are those personal and property rights recognized by a government and guaranteed by a constitution and laws. For example, the Bill of Rights of the U.S. Constitution is a list of rights, such as the freedom of religion and the freedom of speech, that each person enjoys and that cannot by violated by the government.)

Carrying a half-fare military pass, Tubman boarded a northbound train in Washington. The white conductor who looked at the pass refused to accept it. Tubman later told the story to her first biographer, Sarah Bradford. "Come, hustle out of here!" shouted the conductor. "Niggers," he said, were not allowed to travel at reduced rates. When she protested, he grabbed her arm and said, "I'll make you tired of trying to stay here." With three other men, the conductor then dragged Tubman out of the passenger car. The train's white passengers watched in silence. No one helped Tubman as the four large men dragged her to the baggage car and threw her in.

After Tubman rescued her parents in Maryland, she brought them to this house in Auburn. Harriet lived in the house, which is still standing today, for more than 50 years.

Tubman rode north alone, cradling a severely sprained arm. She probably saw the irony of the incident: The woman who had led troops in battle for the Union, the daring rescuer who had escaped bullets, bloodhounds, and angry slave owners, had suffered her first war injury *after* the war—from a civilian in the "free" North.

Tubman experienced continual money problems. She had carefully saved her receipts and records from the war years, and using these documents, Tubman asked her friends to help her figure out how much money the U.S government owed her. They calculated that the government owed her $1,800 for her military services. Tubman desperately needed the money to support herself, her parents, and others who were very poor. Her friend William H. Seward, who was secretary of state, petitioned Congress on her behalf, but nothing happened. Her case came under no official law. Congress refused to recognize the rights of this black woman who had worked so hard and fought so bravely for her country.

In Auburn, Tubman's home was a refuge for many poor blacks who passed through the area looking for work and a home. She fed the hungry, nursed the sick, and helped deliver babies. She also raised money to support schools for newly freed blacks in the South, but her own money situation became desperate. When Sarah Bradford published a biography of Tubman called *Scenes in the Life of Harriet Tubman* in 1869, she turned the profits from the book over to Tubman. The $1,200 helped her greatly.

In 1870, Tubman married a tall, handsome man named Nelson Davis. Some years earlier, Tubman had met him at a South Carolina army base. Even though Nelson had come down with *tuberculosis* during the war and was unable to work at all during their 19-year marriage, he and Harriet remained happily married until Nelson's death in 1888. Ironically, Harriet received funds from Nelson's army *pension* after his death but never was rewarded for her own courageous service to the government.

In these years, Tubman earned her living as a peddler, traveling from house to house and selling vegetables from her garden. Neighbors welcomed her. They gave Tubman something to eat and tea with butter to drink. Then they would listen to her impressive stories of the Underground Railroad and the Civil War.

Queen Victoria, the ruler of Great Britain, was also inspired by Harriet Tubman's bravery. In 1897, she sent Tubman a silver medal and a letter inviting her to come to England. Tubman never visited England, but her friends later reported that she looked at the queen's letter so often that it "was worn to a shadow."

A woman long admired by Tubman was Susan B. Anthony, who was a leader in the women's rights movement. Called *suffragists*, the movement's participants were fighting for the right of women to vote and for other rights that they did not have at the time. (Women did not have the right to vote in the United States until 1920.) Although Anthony never met Tubman,

Suffragists Elizabeth Cady Stanton (left) and Susan B. Anthony pose for a photographer around 1880. Although Tubman never met Stanton or Anthony, she encouraged them in their fight for the right of women to vote.

Anthony returned Tubman's respect by referring to her as "this most wonderful woman." When asked if she really believed that women should have the right to vote, Tubman said, "I suffered enough to believe it."

As Tubman grew older, she became more and more determined to establish a home for sick and needy blacks. In 1896, a 25-acre public lot came up for auction across the road from her house. Tubman was the highest bidder at the auction, promising to pay $450 for the land. She got the money by going to the bank right after the auction and using the land she had just bought as security for a loan. Still, she did not have the money to build the home. Seven years later, in 1903, she gave the land to the African Methodist Episcopal Zion Church, an all-black congregation at which she had worshiped for years. The church built the home in 1908. Tubman was delighted to see the first residents move in, but she was not happy when the home's managers decided to charge an admission fee.

"When I gave the Home over to Zion Church," she told a local reporter, "what do you suppose they did? Why, they made a rule that nobody should come in without a hundred dollars. Now I wanted to make a rule that nobody could come in unless they had no money. What's the good of a Home if a person who wants to get in has to have money?" Tubman and the church finally reached a compromise, and in 1911, she herself moved into the home.

Tubman's final two years were spent in good health at the home, sitting with the visitors and telling exciting stories. In 1913, she told an old friend who had called on her "of the sweet spirit in that home, and of the happiness she felt was there." As the friend was about to leave, Tubman reached for her hand. Holding it tightly, she expressed her hope for the suffrage movement. "Tell the women," said Tubman, "to stand together."

A few weeks later, on March 10, 1913, Harriet Tubman died of pneumonia at the age of

93. Friends who had gathered at her bedside joined hands and sang her favorite spiritual, "Swing Low, Sweet Chariot." The community gave Tubman a military funeral, led by local Civil War veterans. The old soldiers stood at attention, a bugler played taps, and the U.S. flag waved in the breeze.

Today, Harriet Tubman is remembered mostly for her daring work on the Underground Railroad, through which she guided hundreds of slaves to freedom. She was also a skilled military leader, a compassionate nurse, a committed abolitionist, and a woman who cared very much about other human beings. Harriet Tubman, who carried the scars of slavery throughout her long life, devoted her every breath to securing freedom for all people.

Further Reading

Other Biographies of Harriet Tubman

Bentley, Judith. *Harriet Tubman.* New York: Watts, 1990.

Ferris, Jeri. *Go Free or Die: A Story About Harriet Tubman.* Minneapolis: Carolrhoda, 1988.

Klingel, Cindy. *Women of America: Harriet Tubman.* Mankato, MN: Creative Education, 1987.

Petry, Ann. *Harriet Tubman: Conductor on the Underground Railroad.* New York: Archway, 1971.

Sterling, Dorothy. *Freedom Train: The Story of Harriet Tubman.* New York: Scholastic, 1987.

Related Books

Freedman, Russell. *Lincoln: A Photobiography.* New York: Ticknor & Fields, 1987.

McKissack, Patricia, and Frederick McKissack. *Frederick Douglass: The Black Lion.* Chicago: Childrens Press, 1987.

Chronology

ca. 1820   Harriet Tubman is born Harriet Ross on the Brodas plantation in Dorchester County, Maryland.

1835   Harriet suffers a near-fatal blow to the head that leads to lifelong sleeping fits.

1844   Harriet marries John Tubman.

1849   Tubman escapes from slavery to Philadelphia, Pennsylvania, where she befriends abolitionist leaders.

1850   Tubman makes the first of 19 trips into the South as a conductor on the Underground Railroad.

1851   Unable to work safely in the North because of the Fugitive Slave Act, Tubman moves to St. Catharines, Canada.

1857   Tubman rescues her parents from slavery and settles in Auburn, New York.

1858	Tubman meets abolitionist John Brown.
1861	Tubman travels to South Carolina to work with the Union army as a nurse.
1863	Working as a spy for the Union army, Tubman leads a raid up South Carolina's Combahee River, freeing more than 750 slaves.
1869	*Scenes in the Life of Harriet Tubman* by Sarah Bradford is published.
1870	Tubman marries Nelson Davis.
1888	Nelson Davis dies of tuberculosis.
1897	Tubman receives a medal from Queen Victoria of England.
1908	Using land that Tubman had donated in 1903, the African Methodist Episcopal Zion Church builds a home in Auburn, New York, for sick and elderly blacks.
1911	Tubman moves into the home.
1913	Harriet Tubman dies of pneumonia.

Glossary

abolitionist a person who supported the movement to abolish, or end, slavery and the slave trade in the United States

auction a public sale in which goods are sold to those who offer the most money

bounty hunter a person who tracks down and captures outlaws in return for a reward

compass an instrument with a magnetic needle that is used to tell direction

concussion an injury to the brain caused by a fall or a hard blow to the head

contraband goods illegally brought into or taken out of a country; during the Civil War, an escaped slave who fled to or was taken to Union camps

76

Mason-Dixon line   the boundary between Maryland and Pennsylvania, that before the Civil War became known as the border between the slave states of the South and the free states of the North

pension   a sum of money that is paid regularly to a person who has retired from work

plantation   a large farm on which crops, such as cotton, tobacco, or sugar, are grown and harvested

Quaker   a member of the religious group the Society of Friends, which was established in 17th-century England and which believes that no priest or ritual is needed to communicate with God; Quakers believe in the equality of all men and women, and they oppose war

spiritual   a deeply emotional and religious folk song that became a musical tradition among American blacks in the South

suffragist   a person who worked to get voting rights for women

treason   the crime of betraying or plotting against one's country, especially by helping an enemy during a war

tuberculosis   a contagious disease caused by a very small organism that injures primarily the lungs

Index

Bree Burns is a New York–based writer and editor. She is the author of *The Cowboy Storyteller* and has written for magazines and newspapers, including *Back Stage, Theatre Crafts,* and *American Theatre.*

Picture Credits

The Bettmann Archive: pp. 16, 19, 43, 50, 69; Culver Pictures: p. 9; Library of Congress: p. 38; Louisiana Collection, Tulane University Library, New Orleans, LA: p. 36; The National Archives: pp. 56–57, 59; The National Portrait Gallery, Smithsonian Institution, Washington, DC: p. 55; The Schomburg Center for Research in Black Culture, The New York Public Library, Astor, Lenox and Tilden Foundations: pp. 2, 6, 14, 26, 29, 60, 62, 65